My Kind of Family

A Book for Kids in Single-Parent Homes

Michele Lash, M.Ed., A.T.R.
Sally Ives Loughridge, Ph.D.
David Fassler, M.D.

Waterfront Books
98 Brookes Avenue
Burlington, Vermont 05401

ISBN: 0-914525-12-3 (paperback)
ISBN: 0-914525-13-1 (plastic comb spiral)

Library of Congress Catalog Card No.: 90-31471

Designed and produced by Robinson Book Associates
Printed in the United States by Patterson Printing Co.

Contents

On Using This Book

My Kind of Family is about single-parent homes and the people who live in them. The book is written from the child's perspective, incorporating the actual drawings and comments of children between the ages of 6 and 12. Although children may be living in a single-parent home for many different reasons, we have found that they often have similar thoughts, feelings, and questions. We wrote this book to help children express these ideas in a constructive and positive manner.

When sharing this book with a child, it is important to be accepting, flexible, and sensitive to his or her responses. Children should be allowed to explore the book in their own way, covering material in any order and at their own pace. Used in a supportive context, *My Kind of Family* can facilitate open discussion, honest explanation, and shared understanding between children and caring adults.

Acknowledgments

Sarah Bennett
Donna Burnett
Anna Cotton
Billy Cotton
Mary Cotton
Nancy Cotton, Ph.D.
Douglas Dennett, M.D.
Elise Egerter, M.D.
Ann Epstein, M.D.
Ellen Fassler, M.S.W.
Sharon Gordetsky, Ph.D.
Marcia Hemley, Ph.D.
Betsey Ives
Nathaniel Ives
Andrea Lash
Michael Lash

Kelly McQueen
Kathi Newburger, A.T.R.
Sam Loughridge
Sue Niquette
Mimi Pantuhova, Psy.D.
Ava Penman
Joshua Penman
Bill Rae, Ph.D.
David Robinson
Amy Rofman
Julie Rofman
Jennifer Stolz, Ph.D.
Dan Talbert
Kathy Talbert
Morris Wessel, M.D.

and Ashley, Carolyn, Emily, Joseph, Rachel, the students of the
A.D. Lawton School, and the many other children who shared their
thoughts, feelings, and creative expressions.

CHAPTER 1

All Kinds of Families

There are lots of different kinds of families.

Families can be large or small.

Families can include parents, stepparents, grandparents, children, stepchildren, aunts, uncles, nieces, nephews, and cousins.

What do you think a family is?

A family is

at least two People

people living together and
taking care of each other

a mom or a dad and at least one kid

a group of people and their pets

Draw a picture of a family.

I live with my
Mom in an apartment.
We're like a team.

Even though my dad is far away,
he is still part of my family

Families can also have babies.

It takes two people—a man and a woman—to make a baby. Sometimes the man and the woman are married, and sometimes they are not.

Draw a picture of a baby.

18

The Baby

Some kids know both their mom and dad, and some kids don't.

I never met my dad, but I know that he lives in a big city.

Some kids are part of more than one family.

most of the time I live with my mom but when I stay with my dad and his wife, I'm part of that family too.

Draw a picture of your family.

CHAPTER 2

My Kind of Family

Some kids live with both their parents. Others may live with just one. A child who lives with a single parent is part of a single-parent home.

Single means:

just one

by yourself

a first base hit

Not married

Parent means:

a grown up who takescare of you

the person you live with who
makes the   rules

yourmom or dad

the person who signs your report card

Single-parent homes can come about in many different ways.

- Parents may get divorced.

- A parent may die.

- A child may be adopted by a grownup who is not married.

- One parent may not get married to the other parent.

- A parent may move out of the house.

- A woman may decide to have a baby, but not live with the baby's father.

- A child may live with a relative if neither parent can take care of him or her.

My parents used to fight a lot then they got a divorce.

I live with my mom.
My dad died when
I was little.

My mom really, really wanted a baby. I'm glad she decided to adopt me.

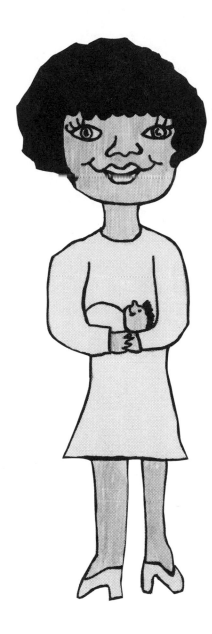

How did you get to be in a single-parent home?

Draw a picture of the people who live in your home.

I think I have a good
kind of family

45

CHAPTER 3

Living in a Single-Parent Home

Lots of kids live in single-parent homes.

Single-parent homes are just like other kinds of homes in many ways.

We all do things together
and help each other.

I help my mom make Pies.

I love everyone in my Family. EXcept sometimes my brother. He can be a real Jerk.

My Mom brings me Soup
When I'm Sick.

I like to go places with my Dad

Some things may be different in a single-parent home.

My dad makes me lunch and takes me to school.

My mom's like a mom and a dad. She does lots of things. She makes me breakfast, goes to work, and takes me to baseball practice.

Sometimes my mom has to work late and I make my own dinner.

ZAP

61

Some things are harder in a single-parent home.

If my dad's busy, there is no one else to go to.

Mom gets tired doing every thing for me and my brother.

My Dad is not so good at picking out my clothes. He's got weird taste.

Single-parent homes have lots of rules, just like other kinds of families.

Rules at home

Don't let strangers in.
Keep clean.
Call Mom for help.
Put the Chain on the door.
Put your toys away.

What are some of the rules in your home?

Kids in single-parent homes have lots of jobs, just like kids in other kinds of families.

What are your jobs at home?

Draw a picture of yourself doing a job.

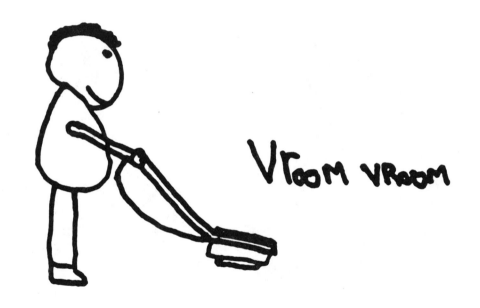

Vroom vroom

I like to help wash the car

Kids in single-parent homes also like to have fun, just like kids in other kinds of families.

It's fun to play with my friends.

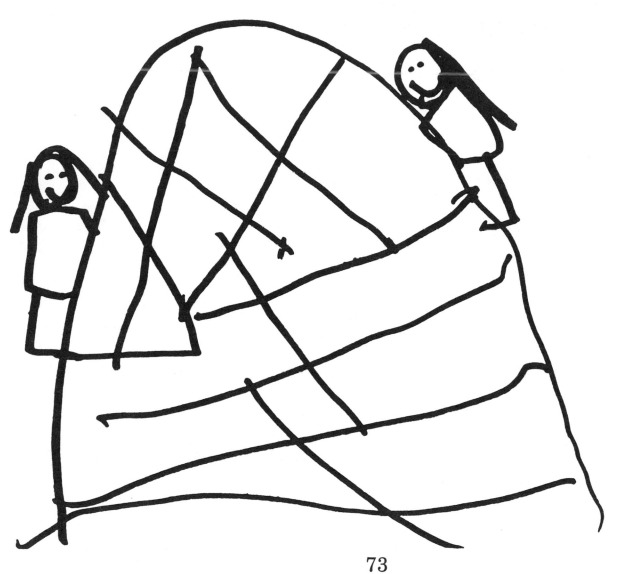

It's fun to go to the beach

Sometimes I have fun by myself.

I am doing a puzzle

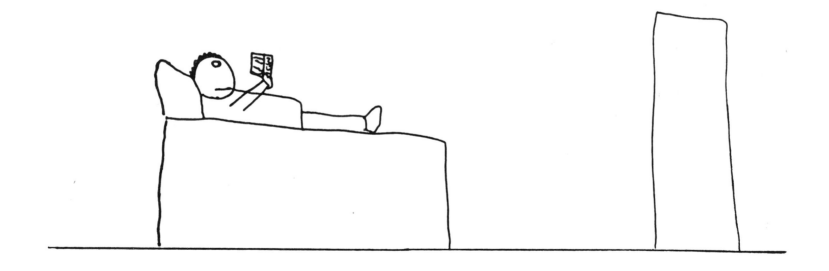

Draw a picture of yourself doing something fun.

81

Eating at Mc Donalds with the rich and Famous

CHAPTER 4

Thinking About Your Other Parent

Everyone starts out with a mom and a dad.

Draw a picture of one of your parents here.

Draw your other parent here.

Even if you don't know your other parent, draw what you think that person might look like.

Lots of kids in single-parent homes think about their other parent and wonder what he or she might be like.

I'll bet my dad is really big and strong.

Maybe my mom is a movie Star

MAYBE my mom is a cop

I 'll bet my mom flies an airplane

I think I saw my dad on TV

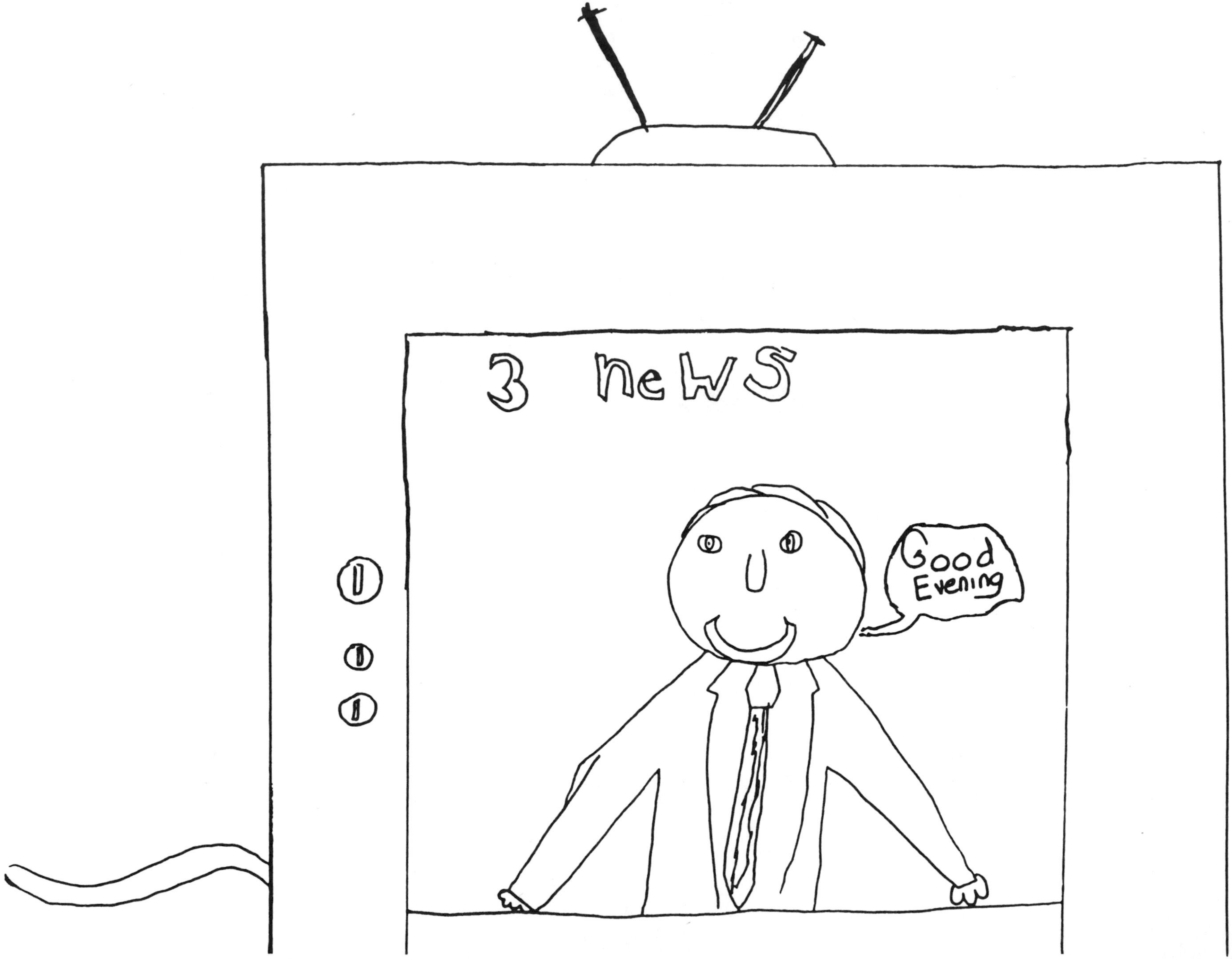

Kids also have lots of thoughts and questions about their other parents.

Why did mom leave?

I wonder if I have other brothers or sisters.

will dad ever come back?

I hope my dad's OK!

Will I ever get to meet my mom?

Does DaD miss me?

What questions do you have about your other parent?

I love my dad, but I still think about my mom a lot.

103

CHAPTER 5

Family Changes

Single-parent homes can go through many kinds of changes.

Some changes are hard and some are easy. Some feel good and some are not much fun.

Mom and I have been on our own for a long time. Now she has a boy friend.

110

My mom's friend Becky came to live with us.

We had to move to a different
apartment.

I'm going to a new school!

Public School

My dad Just got married.

It Feels a little weird.

Mom lost her job. Now she says I
can't get new basketball sneakers.

My dad started going to school at night. He's got lots of homework.

my dad and his girlfriend just broke up.

My mom adopted another baby.
Now I have a little sister.

What changes have taken place in your family?

Draw a picture of a change.

What other changes do you think might happen?

Maybe my dad will get married

Maybe he won't

What changes do you hope might happen?

MAY be I'll Get a new cat.

Maybe my brother will stop being such a Jerk.

Maybe my mom will get a new job.
Then I can get my basketball sneakers.

CHAPTER 6

Feelings, Worries, and Wishes

Kids can have lots of feelings about living in a single-parent home.

Circle some words that show how you feel. Add any others you wish.

• loved	• sad	• mixed up	• weird
• safe	• lonely	• ignored	• jealous
• lucky	• different	• worried	• tired
• normal	• angry	• embarrassed	• scared
• spoiled	• happy	• grouchy	• relieved
• _____	• _____	• _____	• _____

Draw a picture of a feeling.

138

Kids can have other kinds of feelings, too.

I don't like it when my dad has to work on the weekend. Saturday is supposed to be our special day.

I used to live with my mom and my dad. They had lots of fights. Now I live just with mom. I miss my dad, but at least there's no more fighting.

I get sad when my mom comes home late. I don't like staying with the babysitter.

When I fight with my sister, I always get in trouble. It's not fair. She starts it.

Draw a picture of something that makes you mad.

Draw a picture of something that makes you happy.

Draw a picture of something that makes you sad.

Kids in single-parent homes worry about the same kinds of things that other kids worry about. They may also have some worries that are different.

I don't know what to say
when my friends ask about my dad.
I never even knew him.

When my dad yells at me, I worry he might leave like mom did.

153

My dad died 4 years ago. I live with my mom and little sister. Sometimes I worry about mom dying too. What would happen to me?

I worry that my dad will get really old.

Sometimes I worry mom will get lonely.

I worry that my mom won't pick me up from school on time.

I worry that my dad drinks too much.

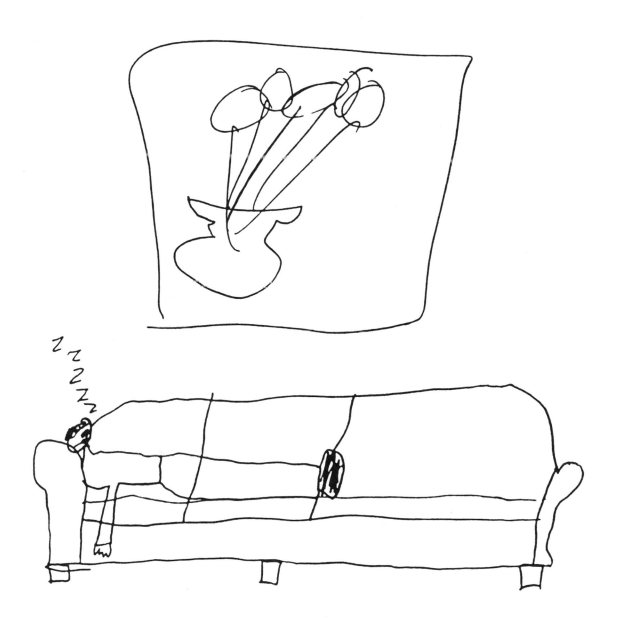

159

What kinds of things do you worry about?

Draw a picture of a worry.

Kids in single-parent homes also have lots of wishes.

My dad and I have Lots of fun, but I still wish I knew my mom.

I wish mom and dad were still married.

I wish I had a puppy

Draw a picture of a wish.

Draw a picture of another wish.

I wish I had a million wishes

169

CHAPTER 7

Growing Up

Kids have lots of ideas about growing up.

Draw a picture of yourself grown up.

What would you like to be when you grow up?

I want to be a teacher

I want to work with animals

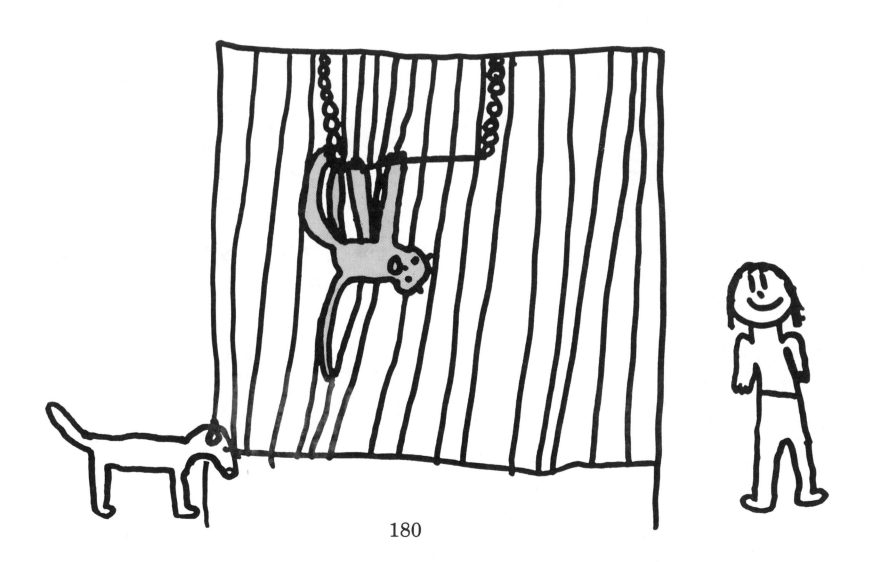

I want to work in an office

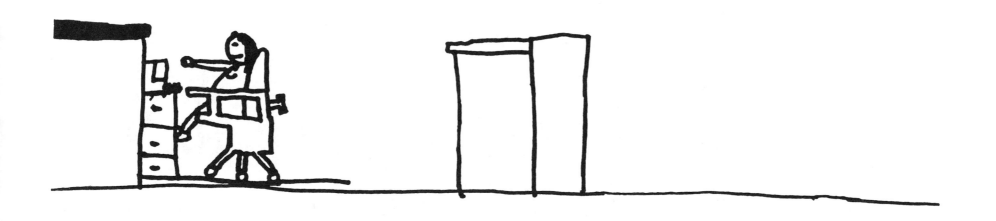

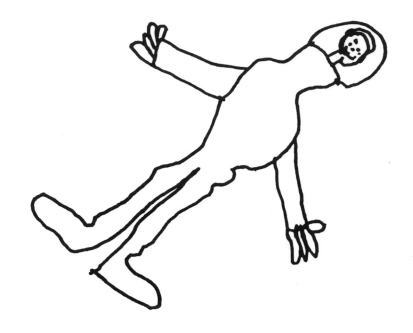

I want to Be an astronaut.

Kids also have lots of questions about growing up.

Where will I live?

What kind of car will I have?

Will I have lots of friends?

Will I get married?

Who will I marry?

Will I have kids?
How many?

Will I have enough money?

Will I be happy?

What are some of your questions about growing up?

When I grow up I'll have
my own kind of family

190

These pages are for you to make up stories or poems or draw any other pictures you want.

Resources

Books for Children

Dolmetsch, P. and Shih, A. *The Kid's Book About Single Parent Families.* New York: Doubleday, 1985.

Evans, M. *This is Me and My Single Parent.* New York: Brunner/Mazel, 1989.

Gardner, R. *The Boys and Girls Book About One Parent Families.* New York: Bantam Books, 1983.

Gilbert, S. *How to Live With a Single Parent.* New York: Lathrop, Lee and Shepard Books, 1982.

Lindsay, J. *Do I Have a Daddy?* Beuna Park, Ca: Morning Glory Press, 1982.

Simon, N. *I Wish I Had My Father.* Chicago, Ill.: Albert Whitman and Company, 1983.

Stanek, M. *I Won't Go Without a Father.* Chicago: Albert Whitman and Company, 1972.

Zindel, P. *I Love My Mother.* New York: Harper & Row, 1975.

Books for Parents

Ciborowski, P. *Survival Skills for Single Parents.* Port Chester, New York: Stratmar Educational Systems, Inc., 1988.

Gatley, R. and Koulack, D. *Single Father's Handbook: A Guide for Separated and Divorced Fathers.* New York: Anchor Books, 1979.

Geddes, J. *How to Parent Alone: A Guide for Single Parents.* New York: Seabury Press, 1974.

Hope, K. and Young, N. (eds.) *Momma: The Sourcebook for Single Mothers.* New York: New American Library, 1976.

Klein, C. *The Single Parent Experience.* New York: Avon, 1983.

McFadden, M. *Bachelor Fatherhood: How to Raise and Enjoy Your Children as a Single Parent.* New York: Walker and Company, 1974.

Weiss, R. *Going It Alone: The Family Life and Social Situation of the Single Parent.* New York: Basic Books, 1979.

About the Authors

Michele Lash received her M.Ed. in expressive art therapies from Lesley College. She is currently affiliated with the Graduate Art Therapy Program at Vermont College. A registered art therapist and psychoeducational consultant, she is in private practice in Essex Junction, Vermont.

Sally Ives Loughridge is a child psychologist practicing in Burlington, Vermont. She received her Ph.D. from the Department of Human Development and Family Studies at Cornell University. A clinical associate professor of psychiatry at the University of Vermont, Dr. Loughridge is also a nationally certified school psychologist (NCSP) and listed in the National Register of Health Service Providers in Psychology.

David Fassler is a child psychiatrist practicing in Burlington, Vermont. A graduate of the Yale University School of Medicine, Dr. Fassler received his training in adult psychiatry at the University of Vermont, and in child psychiatry at the Cambridge Hospital, Harvard Medical School. He is currently a clinical assistant professor and the director of continuing education in the Department of Psychiatry at the University of Vermont, and an instructor in psychiatry at Cambridge Hospital, Harvard Medical School.